Overcoming Fear

Reaching for Your Dreams
and
Knowing Peace of Mind

Dale R. Olen, Ph.D.

A Life Skills Series Book

JODA Communications, Ltd.
Milwaukee, Wisconsin

Editor: Carolyn Kott Washburne
Design: Chris Roerden and Associates
Layout: Eileen Olen

Copyright 1993 by Dale R. Olen, Ph.D.

All rights reserved

ISBN 1-56583-010-5

Published by: JODA Communications, Ltd.
                10125 West North Avenue
                Milwaukee, WI 53226

PRINTED IN THE UNITED STATES OF AMERICA

Table of Contents

	page
Introduction to the Life Skills Series	5
Chapter One: Understanding Fear	9
Chapter Two: The Causes of Fear	15
Chapter Three: Principles and Tools for Overcoming Fear	29
Chapter Four: Developing this Skill with Others	57
Appendix: Review of Principles for Overcoming Fear	61

Introduction
to the
Life Skills Series

Nobody gets out alive! It isn't easy navigating your way through life. Your relationships, parents, marriage, children, job, school, church, all make big demands on you. Sometimes you feel rather ill-equipped to make this journey. You feel as if you have been tossed out in the cold without even a warm jacket. Life's journey demands considerable skill. Navigating the sometimes smooth, other times treacherous journey calls for a wide variety of tools and talents. When the ride feels like a sailboat pushed by a gentle breeze, slicing through the still waters, you go with the flow. You live naturally with the skills already developed.

But other times (and these other times can make you forget the smooth sailing), the sea turns. The boat shifts violently, driven by the waves' force. At those stormy moments, you look at your personal resources, and they just don't seem sufficient.

Gabriel Marcel, the French philosopher, wrote that the journey of life is like a spiral. The Greeks, he observed, viewed life as *cyclical*–sort of the same old thing over and over. The seasons came, went, and came again. History repeated itself. The Hebrews, on the other hand, saw life as *linear*–a pretty straight march toward a goal. You begin at the Alpha point and end at Omega. It's as simple as that.

Marcel combined the two views by capturing the goal-oriented optimism of the Hebrews and the sobering reality of the Greeks' cycles. Life has its ups and downs, but it always moves forward.

To minimize the *downs* and to make the most of the *ups*, you need **Life Skills**. When you hike down the Grand Canyon, you use particular muscles in your back and legs. And when you trudge up the Canyon, you use other muscles. So too with life skills. You call on certain skills when your life spirals down, such as the skill of defeating depression and managing stress. When your life is on an upswing, you employ skills like thinking reasonably and meeting life head on.

This series of books is about the skills you need for getting through life. To get from beginning to end without falling flat on your face and to achieve some dignity and some self-satisfaction, you need **basic** life skills. These include:

1. Accepting yourself.
2. Thinking reasonably.
3. Meeting life head on.

With these three life skills mastered to some degree, you can get a handle on your life. Now, if you want to build from there, you are going to need a few more skills. These include:

4. Communicating.
5. Managing stress.
6. Being intimate.
7. Resolving conflict.
8. Reducing anger.
9. Overcoming fear.
10. Defeating depression.

If you have these ten skills up and running in your life, you are ready to face yourself, your relationships, your parents, your marriage, your children, your job and even God with the hope of handling whatever comes your way. Without these skills, you are going to bump into one stone wall after another. These skills don't take away the problems, the challenges and the hard times. But they do help you dig out of life's deep trenches and more fully *enjoy* the good times.

Life Skills can be learned. You have what it takes to master each of these skills–even if you feel you don't have the tiniest bit of the skill right now. But nobody can develop the skill for you. You have to take charge and develop it yourself. Your family, friends and community may be able to help you, but you are the center at which each skill has to start. Here is all you need to begin this learning process:

- Awareness.
- The desire to grow.
- Effort and practice.

Awareness begins the process of change. You have to notice yourself, watch your behavior and honestly face your strengths and weaknesses. You have to take stock of each skill and of the obstacles in you that might inhibit its growth.

Once you recognize the value of a skill and focus on it, you have to want to pursue it. The critical principle here, one you will see throughout this series, is *desire*. Your desire will force you to focus on the growing you want to do and keep you going when learning comes hard.

Finally, your *effort and practice* will make these **Life Skills** come alive for you. You can do it. These books are tools to guide and encourage your progress. They are my way of being with you— cheering your efforts. But without your practice, what you find in these books will wash out to sea.

Working on these ten **Life Skills** won't get you through life without any scars. But the effort you put in here will help you measure your life in more than years. Your life will be measured in the zest, faith, love, honesty and generosity you bring to yourself and your relationships.

I can hardly wait for you to get started!

Chapter One

Understanding Fear

"If you want to get rid of your fears," the speaker told the attentive audience, "then first get rid of your desires." Try that for a minute. See if you can create a totally "desire-less" environment. Try not looking forward to going on vacation, getting home from work, eating lunch, going to a movie, jogging or sleeping. If you can get free from these simple desires, try ridding yourself of the deeper longings – the desire for companionship, good health, security and, most deeply, for life itself.

Can you do it? No way, right? Do you *want* to do it? Absolutely not! Having desires moves you along. It urges you to take action. Desires, wishes, goals flood your life. They spring to consciousness with almost no prodding. They play a central role in the way you work out your daily living. But – I'm afraid I have to tell you – with those desires come fears. Just as desires and wishes seep into every nook and cranny of your life, so your fears tag right along with them. Fear, like desire, courses through your veins, influencing what you do and don't do.

Think of something you desire. Now, notice, lurking somewhere in a dark corner, the fear. Do you sense it? Pay close attention, because it's there! You plan Mother's Day in the park. The family will gather, bring potato salad and hot dogs, lay out the blankets and have a good, old-fashioned day-long family outing, just like you did when you were kids. You coordinate the event and look forward to the day. But in the back of your mind you wonder if the weather will be warm and sunny. You're afraid it might be cold, windy and rainy. Your bigger fear, however, is whether everyone will get along. There have been occasions when... And what about your cousin who drinks too much?

Defining fear may seem like explaining your fingers. You know what fear is, just as you know that those ten long projections coming out of your hands are fingers. You experience it daily. No one need tell you what in the world it is. But how does it work? How does it sneak up in the first place? What causes it?

Fear arises when you sense impending danger to your personal domain.

Fear always has to do with *possible loss*. Depression occurs when a loss actually takes place. Anger pops up as a way of protecting against a loss. And anxiety or fear surface when you believe a loss in your personal life is imminent. It acts as your "red alert" button. Sirens go off in your body. Blinking lights flash across your brain. All systems go on alert, ready for action.

For example, an important work meeting approaches, called by the Board of Directors of your firm. Your boss asks you to prepare the financial report and present it to the Board. You immediately feel a twinge of anxiety. But you're flattered as well. You know that if you do a good job, the Directors will notice. It could boost your career in this firm. As the day approaches for the meeting, you notice more and more anxiety building up in you. The morning of the meeting you can hardly eat; your stomach is talking to you in six languages.

You're facing a threat to your domain. You fear "goofing up" and *losing* the esteem of the Board and your boss. Your report and the Board's response to it pose a significant threat to your career advancement. Fear rises up. Nothing has actually been lost to you. But the *possibility* of the loss is enough for fear to grab you by the throat. If the fear remains moderate and under your control, it can work *for* you instead of against you. It puts you on your toes and keeps you alert and responsive. It energizes you to be at your best.

However, if the fear becomes overwhelming, it creates a self-fulfilling prophecy. You will act according to your worst fear – which is to fail. Your behavior becomes the product of your own fear.

Panic is an extreme form of anxiety.

You're walking through a shopping mall when all of a sudden a "panic attack" hits you. It springs up from nowhere. Your face flushes. You begin to sweat, grow dizzy and feel faint. Your heart pounds. You wonder if this is the big heart attack. You stagger to a bench and sit down. Yet your heart continues to beat rapidly and your breath comes with difficulty. Worst of all, you feel as though you have no control over what is happening to you.

Welcome to panic attacks. Now, I'm not writing this to worry you. A panic attack doesn't just happen out of nowhere. If you have never had a panic attack before, chances are good you never will. Certain people are more likely to experience such attacks than others. I'll talk about that in the next section.

In a panic attack your body is reacting exactly the way it would during an emergency, with one exception. In panic the response is exaggerated. Recently my wife and I were driving on the freeway when an 18-wheel truck decided he wanted to be in our lane at the same time we were there. So he simply moved over and lightly (as lightly as a semi can do it) bumped the side of our car with his front tire. He knocked us to the side of the road, realized he hit something, swerved back into his original lane and kept right on driving.

Emergency! Emergency! My hands gripped the steering wheel more tightly. My heart beat faster. My breathing got shorter. My concentration intensified. I tried to maintain control, slammed my foot on the brake and slowed down to stop. But he didn't. The emergency intensified. That son of a gun was driving off. I didn't have his license number. So I hit the gas pedal and took off after him. As we caught up, my wife recorded his license number, and I blinked my lights and beeped my horn. He got the message and pulled off the road and stopped. We then took care of business.

In this emergency I had all the same reactions as if I had been in a shopping mall experiencing a panic attack. Only here I felt in control of my body and mind. In the panic attack the panic would control me. On the freeway my heartbeat and rapid body reactions helped me. In the shopping mall those intensified body responses would hinder me.

Certain people are more panic-prone than others.

Will panic strike you when you least expect it? Are you one who may fall victim to its power?

It all depends. People with fear-related characteristics naturally gravitate more toward panic than do calm, easy-going people. A cluster of traits has been identified with people susceptible to panic. If you have these traits it doesn't mean you will automatically receive a call from the panic attacker. You may never get such a call. If you don't have these traits, you can be quite certain you won't wake up in the middle of the night with a panic attack. Here are the characteristics of the typical panic-prone individual:

1. *Low self-esteem:* If you have low self-esteem, you already find it somewhat difficult to believe in your own ability to cope. You tend to be self-critical and to doubt your strength in handling life's

circumstances. You most likely feel like a victim in many ways already. In that fertile field, panic can romp and play to its heart's content.

2. *Tendency to worry:* This seems obvious. If you worry about everything already, you prime yourself for panic. Panic is a ten on the worry scale. So if you have been practicing low-grade worries all your life, eventually you will make it to the big league of worry – a panic attack.

3. *Perfectionist tendencies:* Here's the curse of all anxious people. Everything must be in its proper place and be done absolutely correctly. You know the tremendous pressure this trait puts you under. Most perfectionists admit they are a "little perfectionistic." But what they don't realize is the depth of that tendency. Perfectionism sits in the back of your mind, usually at an unconscious level. Yet it drives all your activity. It's always demanding, insisting that you act a certain way, that you make the rest of the world perfect, that the space and people around you should act perfectly and that the weeds of life should never spring up in your garden.

Because it's pretty hard to make the world perfect, this demanding pressure grows within you, leading to stronger levels of frustration. Eventually the pressure becomes too intense and explodes in the form of a panic attack. Where did it come from, you wonder? From the constant demands you keep making on yourself and others for perfection.

4. *Desire to be a people-pleaser:* This trait spins off from being a perfectionist. Most perfectionists are that way because they want other people to approve of them. They have low self-esteem and learned that if they behave perfectly, others will respond positively. If others are pleased with them, then they can like themselves.

Panic invades people-pleasers because they fear looking foolish to others. They become so self-conscious they cannot attend to anything outside of their own reactions to a situation. Once they have had a panic attack, then, they keep themselves focused on *not* panicking. Of course, that concentration leads to more panic.

5. *Fear of anger and conflicts:* If you fear any of your emotions, you will be prone to panic. You avoid what you fear. By avoiding your feelings, especially the stressful and conflictual feelings, you tend to repress them. You push them into the dark recesses of your unconscious mind. But they still live. They need air. So they gather together and rush out in various ways. One of those ways is panic.

Conflict stands as a normal and fairly common aspect of human life. To be afraid of it causes stress. That stress rubs within you like two earth platelets just before an earthquake. Panic attacks are the psychological tremors that result when stress and conflict are denied and shoved underground.

Chapter Two

The Causes of Fear

Judy couldn't understand it. She woke up in the middle of the night with a major anxiety attack. Her heart was racing. Sweat was pouring off her face. She felt ready to explode. Nothing like this had ever happened to her before. She actually thought she was dying, which scared her all the more. Eventually her heart slowed down and her body temperature returned to normal.

However, the rest of the night she sat in a chair wondering what just hit her. Would it return? What caused this crazy reaction? Was it something she ate? Why couldn't she control it as soon as she woke up? The more questions she considered, the more frightened she became. It was all so new and strange to her. Was she losing her sanity? That would be the worst. She needed answers.

The next morning she called her family physician, who saw Judy that same day. After checking her over, she announced that Judy must have had an "anxiety attack." Judy was shocked. She didn't know she was anxious. Oh, things weren't going so well at work or in her social life. She had been feeling some stress about a special relationship she had with a man. Her parents had been on her case about visiting them more frequently. But she didn't think she was a candidate for panic attacks in the middle of the night.

So how did this major anxiety get started? What could explain it surfacing in Judy's life at this time? I want to offer you, as I did Judy, eight possible avenues to pursue in understanding what causes anxiety. Judy's physician recommended that she see a psychologist. Judy objected, claiming she wasn't crazy. Her physician explained that it wasn't an issue of her being crazy, but an issue of education. She pointed out that fear and anxiety may feel like a psychological or emotional problem, but in most instances they are really *educational* problems. In part, the fear existed because Judy didn't know what was going on. The more she learned, the less fear she would have.

So, too, with you. The more you understand yourself and your fears, the more easily you can overcome them. Let's begin that understanding by looking at the eight causes of fear.

The prospect of death causes anxiety.

Need it even be said? The word "death" itself triggers a slight tightening of the muscles, an increase in the body's alert response and a serious question mark in the mind. You know death must cause great anxiety because the human race spends so much time trying to fight against it, deny it, repress it, question it and understand it.

When people suffer, they want to understand their pain. So they ask "Why?" Undoubtedly, the "Why?" question has been asked more times around death than around any other form of suffering. Understanding reduces fear. The more you understand death, the more you can face it with calm instead of fear. So philosophers, theologians and scientists of every ilk have attempted to offer explanations for death. In fact, many philosophical schemes and almost all religions have been created, in part, to help humans deal with death. The fact that so much emphasis is placed on understanding death clearly indicates that death is a major human preoccupation and a great source of anxiety.

Death causes anxiety because you don't have sufficient information about it and because it threatens your most important possession – namely, your very existence. Everything in you pushes toward continuing to live. The only real threat to that energy for life is death. Death becomes, then, the most frightening force you have to deal with.

Separation causes anxiety.

If you take a trip to a strange city alone, I'll bet you feel more anxiety than taking that trip with a friend. If you journey through life as a solitary figure, you inevitably experience more fear and anxiety than if you walk with others.

Deep within your heart lies an energy for social bonding. When you achieve contact with others, you feel safe and secure. Security does away with fear. In fact, security is the opposite of fear. While frightening realities meet you on the road, having your companion with you gives you a sense of power to overcome the obstacles.

Early in developing relationships both parties fear the loss of the other. They have little security in the relationship. They aren't sure if the other really cares, wants to be in this relationship or might be swept away by some other stunning creature. They even think in very dramatic terms. "I will die if he doesn't call." "There is no point to living if she leaves me." The fear of separation and being alone is so strong that most people go to great lengths to maintain and sustain their growing relationships.

With young children this fear of being disconnected from parents is called "separation anxiety." The baby sitter arrives, and little Timmy wails, screams and pounds the floor with his fists. He can't stand what feels like the loss of Mom. Children in divorcing families often cling to the parent they live with. They have already lost one parent, or so it feels. Now they live with the anxiety of losing the other.

A child who feels unloved or rejected by her parents lives in conflict. She usually experiences some love but not full, unconditional love. This conflict causes anxiety because she suffers a terrible consequence. She grows up without "basic trust." This trust lays the foundation for all future relationships. It allows the child to fully enter relationships because she knows that she is lovable. She can feel confident in her ability to form an intimate relationship and be valued and cherished by another.

Without such basic trust the child experiences a void in the heart. It's as though a piece of her heart was sliced out. Or worse yet, that piece was never developed. The voided heart image looks like this:

If you have experienced the absence of basic trust, then you know the impact of the voided heart. It results in various behaviors, all of which are aimed at filling in what is lacking. Living with a voided heart pushes you toward compensating behaviors. In the old Freudian view such a person was called an "oral personality." This was an individual who could never be satisfied. She constantly searched for completion. She lived her life as a consumer, always taking in, which was where the notion of "oral" came from. Yet no matter how much she took in, nothing satisfied her.

If your heart has been voided by the absent or conditional love of your parents, then you, too, may roam the world, looking for ways to get filled up. You might try filling in the void by eating your way to satisfaction. You might become a workaholic to get filled up. You may enter into the addictive consumption of alcohol or drugs. Any form of addiction can be used as an effort to get filled up, such as hobbies, exercise, cleanliness. You might also become generous to a fault, always doing things for other people, helping whenever possible, often at great sacrifice to yourself.

Finally, to eliminate the voided heart, you may look to other relationships. You may frantically search out relationships anywhere. You take whomever is available. Or you may attach yourself to one person and seek all your fulfillment from that person. Unfortunately, whatever your strategy, it leaves you still with an empty feeling. Something remains missing.

The missing ingredient cannot be found in your present efforts and activities. What's missing happened long ago when you were an infant. Now here's the important realization you need to have about the voided heart: That void, created by the absence of unconditional love, *can never be filled completely again.* The void always remains. The only ones who could have filled that empty place were your parents. And now it's too late. Even if your parents turned their love around, it's the child in you that missed the love.

I know what I just said sounds pretty hopeless. You may be thinking you're doomed to dissatisfaction for the rest of your life. However, you are not. Once you admit you have a voided heart and face that fact, you're on your way to recovery. By realizing you cannot fill up that void, you may experience considerable relief, since now you no longer have to run around the world trying desperately to fill in the empty spot.

That empty place in you is simply a limitation. It's like being born without a right foot. It causes some difficulty at times, but you learn how to live with it, as well as how to work with and around it. Once you give up the quest to fill in that void, you can more gracefully enter other relationships and know intimate love. To a large degree your present and future love experiences actually compensate the earlier void you knew as a child. More about how to work with the voided heart follows in the next chapter.

Seeking approval from others causes anxiety.

While death and traumatic separations may act as the most powerful causes of anxiety, the one that gets you on a day-to-day basis is *approval seeking*. It seeps into the tiniest cracks and crevices of your life. This demon of anxiety has been active in you from childhood and continues with gusto even as you read this.

Think about it for a minute. When you first smiled, slept through the night, cooed, walked, talked, ate with a fork and went on the potty, you received signs of approval from Mom and Dad. At school, teacher's approval came from good grades and a cooperative spirit. Approval came from your peers when you fit in and even at times when you stood out. It gradually became easy to believe that you were a pretty good person *because* others approved of you. If they didn't approve, you felt bad.

Now as an adult the need for approval sneaks into many aspects of your life. You want your house to look nice when the neighbor drops off her son. You don't want to tell the waitress the meat is cold for fear she will judge you negatively. You don't ask your boss for the extra time off because you don't want him to think you're slacking off. At the very beginning of the conversation, you don't tell the telephone solicitor you're not interested because he might get angry with you. Many of these people you don't even know, yet you worry about what they think of you.

When you need other peoples' approval, you live in a state of anxiety. You worry – at least in the back of your mind – about their judgments of you. You become dependent on those judgments for your good feeling about yourself. That's a pretty hefty burden to carry – to rely on what other people think in order to feel good about yourself. Anxiety lies as the bed partner to such dependency.

The step-by-step process of creating anxiety by seeking approval works like this:

1. David has a strong emotional relationship with his mother.
2. Mom sends him approving and disapproving messages based on his behavior.
3. David feels anxious and scared when his mother disapproves. He fears losing her love.
4. To avoid losing her love, David tries very hard to do only those things that will win her approval.
5. Eventually he comes to an important life conclusion: "If I do the right things and do them well, Mom and others will approve of me. If others approve of me, I must be all right. Therefore, I am a worthwhile and good person when I act in ways that make other people pleased with me."
6. David also learns that the more perfectly he behaves, perhaps the more he can guarantee that others will approve. So he becomes a perfectionist, driving himself to always do the very best job possible.
7. This dependence on others' positive evaluations of his work and behavior places him in a vulnerable position. He cannot guarantee others' approval no matter how hard he works at being perfect. Thus, he lives in anticipation and fear of how they will respond to what he does.

A description of this process, in varying degrees, appears daily in therapy offices around the world. The belief that you need other people's approval for your own sense of self lies buried within your developmental process. It seems a natural response to the dynamics of living with loving parents and your youthful need to figure out how to live in this society. Approval and disapproval stand as integral aspects of your lifelong development as a person.

But this very process also causes anxiety, and so needs to be understood and eventually challenged. Although the process of seeking approval is understandable, it is generally not helpful when you become dependent on the approval of others. It generates too much anxiety, which becomes counter-productive in your effort to live a full human life in peace and joy.

The drive to be successful leads to anxiety.

In the section above you saw how success and performance lead to approval by others, which results in approval for self. That places a pretty high price tag, then, on performing well. If you don't, then you won't be worth much.

But success also leads to anxiety. In this culture success itself suggests value, worth, meaning. One of the highest societal values is success. One of the deepest motivational drives is the desire to achieve. That's why people practice their trade, go to school for years, stay late at the office and sacrifice money, time and relationships. When they achieve their goal, they feel completed, whole and satisfied. That end feeling of accomplishment has led many people to great lengths of effort and courage.

As wonderful, fulfilling and energizing as that drive for achievement is, it always carries a flip side. It is laced with anxiety and fear. This is not "bad" anxiety. In fact, it may well assist people in achieving their goals. Some anxiety keeps them on their toes and urges them forward. However, when you feel driven to achieve a particular goal, you need to know that anxiety will accompany you and that you should not let it stop you or overwhelm you in your quest. As I said at the beginning of this book, if you have desires, you will also have fears.

Remember all the fears you had when you were preparing for your first career? You worried about passing school exams, getting the right classes and the right professors, keeping your grade point average in the top quarter of your class. You worried about getting the summer job that would enhance your career direction. You worried about making enough money to get you to that goal. When your studies were completed, you worried about your first interview. Actually you worried about every interview. Once you got the job you felt nervous at evaluation time, you feared your boss's presence, you couldn't sleep the night before your major presentation to the Board and so on.

So with every drive, especially for success, you will feel the fear. Use that fear to spur you on rather than become overwhelmed by it. Fear can stop you dead in your tracks. This drive for success generates your fear of failing. If the fear of failing exceeds your desire for success, then you won't even try to succeed. You will put obstacles and excuses in your way so you won't even have to make the effort.

The fear that attaches to the drive for success can be damaging. It is inevitably present. It must accompany your desire to achieve. That fear can help you or hinder you. For now, simply know it's there, ready to urge you on or stop you from reaching your goals and dreams.

Not having meaning in your life causes anxiety and depression.

Way back in a college philosophy course, I learned people take no action if they have no purpose. You won't get out of bed in the morning if you have no reason to. You won't get into your car and turn on the engine if you have no place to go. You won't go grocery shopping if you don't need groceries. You won't do *anything* if you have no reason to do it.

If you have no meaning in your life, then you will not feel like existing. You will question life itself. You will doubt its value. And you will feel deep within you a threat – a threat to the ending of your own life. That threat will raise a penetrating and abiding anxiety. You will experience a searing conflict between the energy in you to exist, wholly and well, and the lack of reason to exist, the movement toward death. That conflict will frighten you to the core.

Your sense of meaning and purpose rests on three pillars. They are:
1. Work, or the productive use of your time.
2. Relationships with others.
3. A sense of God or some transcendent power or purpose.

These three pillars create and support your sense of meaning in life. They give you reason to get up in the morning and to act throughout the day. Without at least one of these pillars supporting you, the entire structure of meaning in your life comes crashing down.

MEANING AND PURPOSE IN LIFE		
WORK	RELATIONSHIPS	GOD OR HIGHER POWER

Ideally all three of these pillars will stand strong and sturdy throughout your life. They will support you, giving you purpose and energy to live fully and productively. Unfortunately one or the other of these pillars will probably become more significant than the others. You will build it firmly and diligently. The other pillars may, then, be under-built. They will lack the materials and labor to make them strong and supportive beams. With one or two weak beams you set yourself up for anxiety. You become dependent on the one pillar to sustain your sense of meaning. What if it comes crashing down one day?

John found meaning in his work. An architect, he loved creating dynamic and functional buildings. He worked very hard, often referring to himself as a workaholic. He spent every waking hour pouring over designs, graphing out dimensions. Nights, weekends, holidays, vacations all involved his work. Yes, he was married and had three children. He knew he neglected them. He felt badly about it. But his work called him and gave him satisfaction.

Eventually his wife divorced him and took the kids. He felt awful. But he gave himself over to his work even more fully. As the years passed and age began to creep up on John, he found his eyesight being affected by glaucoma. He was going blind. At the same time, arthritis was coursing through his joints, especially his fingers and hands. He couldn't see and he couldn't draw. He was losing his work. Anxiety and depression began setting in. His work pillar was crumbling before his eyes. Finally he had to give up his work. Nothing else meant anything. Alone, without much belief in God or a greater purpose, John's life no longer had meaning. It had come crashing down when his pillar of work crumbled.

Many people do what John did, perhaps in less dramatic ways. They focus on work to give them meaning. When they do so, they suffer the "drive for success" anxiety I talked of above. If their meaning comes from work, then they must be successful. If they aren't, then their work becomes meaningless and so do they.

Other people rely on relationships for meaning. Parents who focus their sense of purpose solely on their children are in for a shock when the kids grow up and leave home. The work pillar or the God pillar needs to stand strongly for these people because their relationship pillar will be shaken.

Not many people make the God pillar their primary pillar. They use it as a back-up. As they age – with their work and relationship pillars weakening – they turn more to the God pillar. Those who do make the God pillar the strongest, to the neglect of their other pillars, eventually experience the "dark night of the soul" and find that pillar shaken as well.

If all three of your pillars are weakened, you experience the crisis of meaning. You feel the anxiety that threatens your very existence. Clearly the response to such a threat needs to be the strengthening of all three of the pillars. Putting energy into each of these areas leads to the balance that supports your sense of meaning in life. Meaning and purpose come from these three sources – work, relationships and God. Having such purpose drives out the threat to your very existence by giving you reason to live.

Basic inner conflicts cause anxiety.

Think of that poor, hungry donkey standing between two bales of hay. What anxiety! He struggles with the pros and cons of going to his left or right. Both look attractive. Both have some negatives. He dies of starvation because he can't decide.

This is called a "double approach-avoidance" conflict. Both sides have elements that make the donkey want to approach. And both have elements that make him want to avoid. Similar conflicts arise within you. On the one hand you seek *independence*. It looks attractive. How nice to be away at school or own your own house or business. How liberating to make your own financial decisions and to feel free from caring what others think about your choices. But such independence can feel lonely at times. It can cause self-doubt. It can lead you to feel unsupported. Independence, then, causes you to both approach it and avoid it.

On the other hand, you seek *dependence*. It looks attractive. You need not make decisions or take responsibility. Let the one you depend on do that. It feels good to be taken care of. All your worries and concerns can be given to the other. You need never leave the warmth of the womb. But you sense you won't grow as a person staying with "Mommy." You remain beholden to the other, always indebted to her. Approach and avoidance.

As you attempt to decide which way to go, anxiety creeps in. You're afraid of choosing independence because of what you might lose in dependence. And vice versa. Think about launching out into a new business venture. You have always wanted to own your own restaurant. You already have a good job as head chef in a very successful establishment. But you're not the boss. You seek independence. You can already feel the anxiety welling up in you as you consider what you have to lose. Whenever you focus on what you *might* lose, you will feel anxious.

Another inner conflict occurs between *individuality* and *community*. You want to be your own person, a unique creature who is clear on who you are and what your boundaries are. On the other hand, you seek union with others. You want to merge your boundaries and become one with that special person. Both create fear. If you're too separated from others, you fear living alone forever. If you merge too deeply with another, you fear losing your unique sense of self. This inner conflict causes anxiety because it raises the scepter of losing something you value.

Such inner conflicts, then, cause anxiety. When these inner conflicts are identified and resolved, you notice the release of anxiety as well.

Feeling like you are losing control causes anxiety.

Why do you feel more anxious on an airplane than driving a car? Why do you feel more anxious when someone else is driving the car than when you are? Because in both of these situations you have less control. The less power you have to create an outcome, the more anxiety you will have in that situation. No matter how strong your legal case appears, when you get into the courtroom, you are not in control of the outcome. You look to the judge and jury. In applying for a new job, you might have all the right credentials, but you don't make the decision. So you can't sleep the night before decision time, filled with anxiety. You want a closer relationship with Linda but don't know if she likes you as much as you like her. You pace the floor nervously all night waiting for her to call you. You don't have control.

Perhaps the most dramatic area in which you want control has to do with your emotions. If your emotions appear to have a life of their own, your anxiety increases. You don't want to go crazy. You don't know what you'd do if that happened. You'd make an absolute fool of yourself. You might find yourself crying at the drop of a hat or feeling rage at the slightest provocation. The sadness you feel penetrates so deeply you conclude there is no way out. These strong, intense emotional reactions scare you because they seem to live and act in you without your consent. They have taken you over. This sense of being out of control adds to the already overpowering feelings that fill you.

One way of overcoming anxiety is through your ability to maintain a sense of control over all aspects of your life. That's why you are probably not afraid to drive a car. When you're driving, you believe you have some control.

Now you know what anxiety is and what causes it. Next I want to share with you concrete ways of facing, fighting and overcoming the fears and anxieties that disable you.

Chapter Three

Principles and Tools for Overcoming Fear

Although I don't much like the words "right and wrong," when it comes to overcoming fear, there is a "right" way and a "wrong" way to do it. Throughout the rest of this book I'm going to tell you the "right" way to overcome fear. But for a moment let me point out the ways *not* to fight fear.

First of all, when you feel afraid, do not get into *frantic activity*. It only increases the intensity of the fear. Observe a group of fans watching a football game on television. It's Super Bowl Sunday. Your team is ahead by two points with three minutes to go, and the other team has the ball. Everyone begins acting frantically. Some people are up and pacing; others are shoving in chips, sandwiches and beer at a breakneck speed; others are leaving the room, coming back in and walking out again. The frantic activity only heightens the anxiety.

Second, do not get trapped by *rigid thinking*. One way of creating certainty is to freeze your thinking. Now you can have no doubts. Not having doubts does away with fear. You can predict the outcome. Unfortunately, rigid thinking doesn't always fit reality, and when it doesn't a major rub occurs. You insist that reality should fit your stiff thinking. You believe that the world must conform itself to your thoughts. When it doesn't, you are in conflict. That conflict, as we saw before, increases your anxiety.

Third, do not try to avoid *anxiety-producing situations*. Not showing up for an appointment, pretending a conflict isn't really happening, or stifling a feeling of sadness are all common ways of avoiding anxiety-producing situations. We call these techniques "denial." Certainly there are times when avoiding scary situations is just fine. If you think sky diving might be dangerous and would cause you anxiety, choosing not to do it makes sense. But denying your fear or attempting to insulate yourself from frightening situations only keeps you focused by your fears, thus heightening them. Remember, you give power to what you focus on. By trying so hard *not* to focus on anxiety, you end up paying a lot of attention to it.

Finally, do not become *extremely cautious and careful*. Again, by being overly cautious you keep yourself focused on the possible dangers. By attending too much to the dangers, you increase them. If I tell you to be really careful about riding that particular elevator, you will feel more fear as you cautiously step onto it, even if there is absolutely nothing wrong with it.

So what should you do with your fears? What are the more helpful ways of managing your anxiety and reducing your fears?

You most effectively control and eliminate your fears by following these four steps:
1. Become aware of your fear and what causes it.
2. Learn to think in non-fearful ways.
3. Take definite action steps.
4. Learn to relax.

I will discuss each of these steps with you in considerable detail below. As is true in working with any emotional or psychological aspect of your life, *understanding* and a lot of *effort* are needed. I will try to bring you some of the understanding and will bank on you bringing the effort needed to learn this skill.

Become Aware of Your Fear and What Causes It

Without doubt the most important step in any psychological process is to increase your awareness. Reading this book immediately helps you do this. It forces you to concentrate on your fears and why they exist. Here are some things to be aware of and some principles and tools to help you develop higher levels of awareness around your fears.

Principle 1

Information increases your ability to predict outcomes. Predictability reduces fear.

Jennifer feared flying. It became a source of friction between her and her husband, who loved going on trips. He used those trips as a time to get closer to Jennifer. She wanted to go with him but always found excuses. The fact was, she was scared stiff. She found one solution to dealing with her fear, although she didn't like it. She would drink herself into numbness before and during the flight.

After years of fear Jennifer enrolled in a "Fear of Flying Course" at the airport in her city. It was a four-week course, offered by a psychologist. Although he taught some relaxation techniques, he spent most of the time explaining the parts of an airplane, how a plane works and the principles involved in keeping a plane in the air despite its 2,000 pounds of mass. The last class involved a flight to another city. Fortunately, or unfortunately, it was a stormy night. The flight was bumpy. But Jennifer went. She felt much less fearful than she ever had before, even though this flight was the worst she had ever experienced. She reported that knowing so much about how the plane worked gave her the confidence it would make it.

The more information you have, the better able you are to predict the outcome of an event. If you know how an event will end, you experience very little anxiety, right? If you know that the villain in the movie jumps out at the woman walking down the street, you're not scared when it happens. If you know how you scored on the final exam, you don't worry about the grade on your report card. (You may be depressed about it, but you don't worry.) If you know she will say "yes" when you ask her to marry you, it doesn't cause you anxiety during the romantic supper before you pop the question.

Stanley Rachman, a professor of abnormal psychology, wrote as much in his book *Fear and Courage* (W.H. Freeman and Co., 1978). "The more information we have about the nature of the expected aversiveness . . . the greater the likelihood that we will find ways of preventing it from occurring or of reducing its consequences if it does occur."

He's talking about situations that would naturally cause you to be afraid. For example, suppose you have to go to the radiologist for an Intravenous Pyelogram. This is a test where a doctor shoots a dye into your vein so she can take pictures of your kidney, ureter (the tube running from the kidney to the bladder) and bladder. If you're informed only that this test must be done and you have no other information, then you have no way of predicting how painful and uncomfortable the test will be. And if you have no idea why your doctor wants this test done, you also will not be able to anticipate its results.

Without such information you can easily begin guessing at how painful the test will be and its possible awful results. Your anxiety reaches mammoth proportions before you even get to the hospital for the test. But if the doctor explains the entire procedure and exactly what she is looking for, then you can let go of much of your fear, especially if the information given indicates the only discomfort will be the needle prick. Knowing in advance what you're getting into helps you predict the outcome. Usually such information helps reduce your anxiety.

So seek as much information as you can about potentially scary events. Such information reduces your tendency to dramatize the outcomes and helps keep you in the real world. Being able to predict the outcome, based on information and not just on your wild guesses, helps you lower your anxiety level considerably.

Principle 2

Create an attitude of courage by viewing yourself as competent.

Courage counteracts fear. Studies of "courageous people" indicate that they see themselves as capable of matching up to the task at hand. They think they can cope with any difficult situation and get through it, even if it will be tough or painful.

If you don't feel very courageous, think of how many life situations you have already come through successfully. You've done just fine. You have managed very well, and you will continue to do so in the future. Remember going to school for the first time? Tough, but you did it and survived. It was harder when you moved and had to go to a new school in fifth grade. But you got through that all right, too. Even though when you were a teenager the kids teased you about being overweight, you survived that and became very sensitive, in fact, to other young people who are overweight.

Remember the first time you caddied at the country club. You were so afraid the golfer would be displeased with you. But after a couple of holes you felt confident, as though you had been born to caddie. You were afraid when you took your driving test but did just fine. Fear gripped you when you went to college, when you got your first "real" job, when you walked up the aisle and said "yes." You acted courageously when you decided to have children (perhaps foolishly, but courageously nonetheless!). And it took a great deal of courage when you bought the house and mortgaged away your life.

Keep in mind how hard it was when your best friend moved to the other end of the country. You're still making that relationship work, even though it demands more time and money with those long-distance calls and plane trips once a year. And yes, you've even made it through your father's death, which you never thought you'd be able to handle.

Come to think about it, you really have been a very courageous person. Can you handle what's ahead of you? Most definitely yes! I believe it. Over the years I've heard many people tell incredibly tragic and difficult stories and they are making it. Certainly there are scars. But these people have more courage than even they imagined. You do, too. Take a quick trip through your life, acknowledging all the acts of courage you've already completed. You've done it in the past, you can continue to act with courage in the future. You will make it through the tough times. This you need to believe.

Principle 3

Focusing on who you are rather than what you do helps reduce anxiety.

You've heard it since you were little: "It's not so important what you do. It's who you are that counts." But you didn't believe it. You may have nodded your head, but you knew, deep in your heart, that it's what you do that matters. What is this "being stuff" anyway?

That trite saying is actually true. It's just not understood well. People who feel good about themselves experience less anxiety than people who don't like themselves or people who aren't sure of themselves. And people who like themselves base their self-approval on something within rather than on their behavioral accomplishments. Those are too fleeting and unstable. You need to base your self-esteem on *being,* on something inside of you, and not on *doing,* not on your successes and your wonderful accomplishments. Remember, fear arises from the *threat* of losing important elements of your personal domain. The greatest threat is the attack on your identity and your existence. So to protect yourself from such threats, you need a self-concept that is immune from destruction. You need a sense of self that cannot be shaken, that doesn't depend on your achievements and the opinions of others. You need total confidence that the basis of your self-esteem cannot be touched by any outside forces.

If you have such confidence, you appreciate how much anxiety has been eliminated from your life. Certainly, you might still fear heights and barking dogs, but you don't feel the deep anxiety of losing your entire sense of self.

How to shift from putting your stock in "doing" to "being" takes us beyond the scope of this book. If you have not already read the **Life Skills Series** book *Accepting Yourself,* I would encourage you to do so. It will help you learn ways of re-focusing from doing to being.

For now, let me just say that "being" consists of focusing on basic core energies that lie deep within you. These energies come with human life. You possess four basic energies or powers, and these energies are fundamentally good. *You are these energies.* They are the energy to exist, the energy to exist as best and as fully as you can, the energy to be free and the energy to love. If you pay close attention to yourself, you will notice these movements deep within you. These movements or energies make you *be* who you are. You may not always *act* or *do* according to these energies, but the energies remain.

These energies are constant. They cannot be taken from you by anyone or anything. They are immune from any threat. They are givens. No matter what happens in your life, you continue to possess these four powers. You are your energies. And since they are good, so are you.

The flip of that is you are *not,* then, your behaviors. You are also not your feelings or your thoughts. And most certainly you are not other people's opinion of who you are. You are the energies of your heart! No one, nothing, can touch or threaten those basic energies.

Your ability to focus on those energies – your being – rather than your doing can help you reduce anxiety and fear in your life. By accepting yourself as a good person who cannot be threatened at your core, you eliminate a major source of anxiety. You no longer need to fear the loss of yourself.

Principle 4

Make an act of faith in your own nurturing power to handle your "voided heart."

Recall that in the section of this book on "Causes of Fear" I talked with you about the "voided heart." If you are not loved deeply as a child, you now have an empty place in your heart. You attempt to fill that void in a wide variety of ways. But none of them completely satisfies you. The constant search creates anxiety. To overcome this anxiety and the basic dissatisfaction with life, you need to take a few steps:

1. Explore with another person your childhood relationship with your parents. Allow your feelings to surface. Whatever is buried regarding your parents needs a chance to become conscious. Recognize that much of your "filling up" behavior today is being influenced by your childhood wishes for parental love. Once you realize that, you can then make a choice to continue acting out of the child in

you, or you can choose to respond out of an adult stance that acts against those childhood beliefs.
2. Realize that your voided heart can never be filled again as completely as the child in you would like. This realization is painful, but helps you let go of all the frantic behavior you have used to get filled up. Relief replaces dissatisfaction. Further, you need not give up your hope for a fulfilling and happy life. Although your heart has an empty place (which could only have been filled in your childhood by your parents), you can still know adult love.
3. Make an act of faith in your own inner goodness. This is a deliberate, conscious choice you make to believe that you are lovable and good despite the lack of love you received early on. Such a conscious choice doesn't necessarily *feel* convincing. But then an act of faith, in part, means believing without feeling or having proof. Even though you may feel unlovable at times, you can insist that you are a valuable, lovable person.

You regularly make acts of faith in bridges, even though you feel uncomfortable walking across them. You make an act of faith every time you get in your car, especially in a snow storm. You make an act of faith regarding life after death, despite the fact that you often have doubts about what happens when you die. Here too, then, you need to make an act of faith that you're a lovable, worthwhile person even though you sense the void in your heart.

Principle 5

Search for answers to the ultimate questions of life.

Anxiety grows when you're not sure what your life is all about. If you don't have some satisfactory view of life that helps you explain why you're here and what your ultimate purpose is, then you will have anxiety. If you have a vague sense about where you are headed on your summer vacation, you will have anxiety about your destination.

When painful events occur in your life, such as the death of a close relative or the loss of a lifelong job, you look for answers to explain the pain. You try to make sense out of the loss. If you cannot figure out the meaning of your pain, you gradually fill up with anxiety because you don't have control over what happened. When you can explain something, you feel as though you have some power over it. Information brings you safety. So you attempt to make sense out of tragic and painful life experiences.

You also try to make sense out of the daily events of life. While driving to work for the 20,000th time, you begin to wonder what in the world you keep doing this for. What is the point of it all? of life? of work? of love? of children? of death? Without some answers to these questions, you feel out of control with life itself. Whenever you feel that loss of control, you will know anxiety.

Most people seek some cosmic or religious view of creation to help explain the meaning of it all. Throughout the ages philosophers and theologians have attempted to explain the purpose of life and death. Most children are raised in families replete with religious views of the world. But what you learned as a child may no longer satisfy you now. As an adult you need more thoughtful answers. To find those, you need to dig deeper. It takes work, reflection and discussion to penetrate the mysteries of life.

To make some sense out of life, you need to read, think and talk. As people you love die, you are forced to ask yourself all the life-death questions. The answers seem a little more muddy. You have some doubts. But you need to continue the search to make sense out of life. As you do, a certain contentment settles within you. Being able to say, "Yes, that makes some sense," yields peace of mind and banishes fear.

Don't be afraid of facing these questions as an adult. Confront them. Even though you may only discover partial answers, you will find yourself more able to say "yes" to life and to death.

Learn To Think In Non-Fearful Ways

Your best remedy for fighting fear lies in your mind. Although it *feels* awful, fear first happens in your *thoughts*. By changing your view of a situation, you alter your reactions and feelings to it. Certain types of thoughts generate anxiety quickly. By recognizing those thoughts, you have the opportunity to challenge them and change them to less frightening thoughts.

Principle 6

Recognize and challenge dramatic and catastrophic thinking.

If you think in dramatic ways, you generate fear. Of course, you probably don't see yourself as a dramatic thinker. You believe all your thoughts fit perfectly with reality. But herein lies the problem. Because you believe you're in touch with reality, your dramatic thoughts are interpreted by you as realistic.

But just because you think you're viewing the world in a realistic way does not mean you actually are. The proof of your dramatizing lies in the amount of worrying you do. In other words, if you worry frequently, I guarantee you're thinking in dramatic ways, out of touch with reality. If you find yourself in a state of fear or worry, then begin by doubting the accuracy of your beliefs. They are off-center. By starting with a doubt, you give yourself an opening to view the situation in a more calm and positive light.

You thought, for example, that you and your co-worker, Alice, were friends. You worked together for eight years. A certain warmth and affection passed easily between you. But yesterday morning, she became angry with you – the first time you ever recall that happening. She snapped at you about not pulling your load. Then she stalked off.

All day, you didn't see her. But your mind was working. You knew she was angry at you. Your dramatic thinking began to kick in. You thought she might have been angry at you for a long time, maybe even all eight years. Perhaps she never really liked you but just tolerated you. She was probably jealous of your success and is now trying to cut you down. As you thought these dramas throughout the day, they became more real. This morning, as you awake, your anxiety is up and dressed before you even get out of bed. What will happen when you see her at work today?

When you get to work, Alice appears chipper and good-humored. She greets you pleasantly and immediately apologizes for her little outburst. She explains that she and her teenage son argued about house work just before she came to the office yesterday. She felt used and taken advantage of. She unloaded on you and admitted that wasn't fair.

All your fear about your relationship with Alice now washes away. You realize you wasted the entire day being upset because you dramatized the situation. Your thoughts caused your anxiety. If from the beginning you had doubted your dramatic thoughts, you could have replaced them with more realistic thoughts, such as, "Alice must be upset about something else and is unloading it on me. That's the sign of a true friendship."

Pay attention today to your dramatic thinking. Words such as "always" and "never" suggest exaggeration and drama. Inflating numbers is dramatic: "I've told you a million times . . . " Watch your inner and outer language and listen for these cues. Notice how quickly you think in catastrophic terms: "I can't stand the dentist's drill." "I'll never understand this material and will flunk the class for sure." "The IRS is sure to audit us and will make us pay thousands of dollars in taxes we missed." On it goes. Simply attend to the dramas and catastrophes that occur in your mind but usually not in the real world.

You learned to think dramatically as a child. To make an impression, parents and teachers taught you in dramatic fashion. The nursery rhymes you learned were filled with drama because their purpose was to teach you right from wrong. Listen to the catastrophe in them: Humpty Dumpty fell off the wall and couldn't be put back together again. Isn't that terrible. Jack broke his crown (his head) and Jill came tumbling after. There were three *blind* mice – I don't know why – who got their tails cut off with a carving knife. London Bridges came falling down; and Jack had to flee the giant in the beanstalk. Your parents put you to bed reciting: "When the bough breaks, the cradle will fall, and down will come baby, cradle and all. Good night, sweetheart." Then they turned out the lights saying: "Sleep tight. Don't let the bedbugs bite."

So challenge your dramatic and catastrophic thinking in order to cut into your fear. You can just as easily believe you have a headache as a brain tumor. You can believe your speech at the PTA meeting will be well-received rather than a flop. You can anticipate your airplane trip going through smooth skies rather than thunderstorms and a tornado. Keep challenging those worrisome thoughts. Realize that about 98 percent of all your worries never come true. Your chances of positive outcomes are pretty good, I'd say.

Principle 7

Make sure you observe data in a calm and accurate way.

The *Observer* in you plays a central role in increasing or reducing your fear. What you observe, how you observe it and the conclusions you come to from your observations all bear on your level of anxiety.

R. Reid Wilson, Ph.D., in his book *Don't Panic* (Harper and Row, 1986), identified three unhelpful Observers:
1. *The Worried Observer:* This is the part of you that anticipates the worst. You see the future with all the awful possibilities looming before you. You expect the catastrophic. Your team can be up by 20 points with one minute left in the game, and you still worry that the opponents can come back and win. You are forever vigilant for any small signs of trouble.
2. *The Critical Observer:* This is the part of you that knocks you down every chance it gets. It makes you feel helpless and hopeless. The Critical Observer says, "What's the use trying. I'm not able to do this anyhow." This Observer reminds you of your past mistakes and how badly you have functioned in similar situations. It likes to identify your flaws and rub your nose in them. Feeling helpless and powerless increases your anxiety.
3. *The Hopeless Observer:* This observing part of you has low self-esteem. It generally expects that you will fail at whatever you do. It anticipates that whatever you touch will turn to coal. It views you as inherently defective. And finally, it believes you will never reach your goals due to insurmountable obstacles, the biggest being *you*.

Again, these observing parts of you need to be challenged and kicked out of your system. To do so, focus on the attributes of a *Healthy Observer*. According to Wilson, the *Healthy Observer*:
1. Takes the time to gather as much relevant information as possible. Gathering information reduces dramatic interpretations.
2. Attempts to get free from strong emotions, since emotions cloud and influence the observing eye.
3. Thinks calmly and quietly, while being concerned.
4. Is as free as possible from prejudices and closed views of

people and situations.
5. Sees the broad perspective in a situation and views it in the context of other events and information.
6. Has mental flexibility to view problems in various ways and from different angles.
7. Attempts to view the event as a detached video camera might record it.

Working to gain these perspectives by consciously practicing them helps reduce the anxiety in your life and allows you to live with greater peace of mind.

Principle 8

Insist on and practice thinking in positive, objective and calming ways.

Fear happens because your mind automatically kicks in frightening beliefs. These beliefs were learned all through your life, and now they pop up whenever a scary situation appears. At this point it takes a conscious effort and a hard fight to identify your fearful beliefs, reject them and insert new, more calming thoughts.

To do this, you need to know what kind of calming, reasonable thoughts you can insert in order to counter the old, more worrisome ones. You cannot simply say to yourself, "OK, I'm thinking very dramatic and catastrophic thoughts about this rain storm, so I'll just stop and tell myself not to worry." That approach, as you know, doesn't work. You need to replace the old thoughts with new, active and positive thoughts. Here are some thoughts people use who are good at managing their fear:

- I can handle this situation.
- I am in control of myself, my feelings and my behavior.
- I am free and have choices to make here.

- I can trust myself to make the best decision.
- I expect a positive outcome and future.
- I have been successful in the past.
- I have good skills and the ability to deal with life.
- What's the worst that can happen? I can manage it.
- I know I can adjust to this change.
- I can always find people to support me.
- I will focus on the solution rather than the problem.
- In the great scheme of things, this issue is not that big.
- I can make my view that of a videotape, thus reducing the subjective and dramatic interpretations I create.

These kind of beliefs, thought regularly and consistently, begin interfering with your old, locked-in, worried beliefs. Gradually these new beliefs become more believable. As they do so, you begin letting go of your old beliefs and begin experiencing the calm and peace that comes when your thinking matches reality. Be ready to work hard on this. The old beliefs don't want to let go. But your efforts will pay off. Your fears will diminish as your thinking becomes positive.

Principle 9

Gain a sense of personal power in your life.

The more you believe in your own power and control, the less fear you have. Fear doesn't keep you from taking action in your life; seeing yourself in a weak, powerless position does. Sure, you may be afraid to go for the job interview, but you'll still go if you think you have a good shot at getting the job. But if you believe the company already picked someone else, you won't even knock on the door. Powerlessness, not fear, stops you from acting.

In order to take power, Susan Jeffers, Ph.D., offers several steps in her book, *Feel the Fear and Do It Anyway* (Fawcett Columbine,

1988).

Avoid casting blame on external forces. As soon as you blame someone or something else for your plight in life, you give up your ability to change the situation. All you can do is continue to demand that the other change. But you have little power to enforce that change. When two people blame each other for the breakdown of their marriage, they remain stuck. They both give up their own power to change the situation and now wait for the other person to shape up. No. You need to keep focused on yourself, on your part in the difficult situation and on what *you* can do either to change the situation or deal with it more effectively.

Don't blame yourself for not feeling in charge. The inmates have taken over the asylum. Or, more pertinent, the kids have taken over the home. You feel you have lost control of your children. They don't listen to you anymore. They do what they want. Emotionally you feel out of control. Your anger jumps out at the least provocation. But worst of all you start blaming yourself for not being in control. What an awful parent you are. You should never have had kids because you're messing up their lives.

It's this last step, blaming yourself for "losing it," that causes you to feel even more powerless. The situation is awful, but now so are you. With that grip on you, it's hard to move. It's as if you were an olympic swimmer who put on a strait jacket just before the final race. Why even bother trying to correct the situation? You're such a bad parent, you've already messed up the kids permanently. Just quit. You can't change them or yourself anyway.

Instead of such hopeless thinking, keep away from any judgment about yourself. Realize the kids have gotten a little wild. You're still the adult here. You have resources within you and around you to cope, manage and correct the situation. Right this second you might not be sure what those resources are, but you can find them. Nobody asked you to sit around and judge yourself as incompetent. Think, instead, of taking action – once you determine what action might work.

Find the payoffs for staying stuck. What do you get for remaining powerless? If you give up the power to change a situation, you probably receive in return a false sense of security. Unfortunately, without a sense of your own power you feel, in fact, more anxiety rather than less. A woman can no longer tolerate her marriage, but she feels powerless to change it or get out of it. She's stuck. What's the payoff? She maintains financial security. At least there's a warm body around. That may seem preferable to being totally alone. She can hang onto her eternal hope of having the ideal marriage. Those are just a couple possible payoffs that might keep her powerless.

By attending to your payoffs, you gain the opportunity to challenge them and line them up against the payoffs that come from taking control of your life. Most of the time the benefits that come from living without power turn out to be shallow blessings. Gaining power in your life and taking risks may trigger some anxiety, but the results of such power tend to lead to richer benefits and a fuller life.

Decide what you want and go for it. Easier said than done. But to feel powerful again, you need to make decisions and then act on them. If you have trouble making decisions, it might be because you perceive the choices in "right-wrong" terms. You think there is a "right and good" decision, and there is a "wrong and bad" decision. Try to get out of that moralistic terminology. Think instead of your decisions as generally occurring between two positives: Should you move to Arizona or stay in Wisconsin? There isn't a right or wrong here. Both can work out. One might work out a little better than the other. But then, no matter what decision you make, you never really know if the other decision would have been a better choice. So you make a decision and give yourself over to it. You view it as a "good" decision, and you make it work. You embrace it. So you choose to stay in Wisconsin. You embrace the snow, the changes of season, the summertime activities and the beauty of fall. What a good choice!

Or you decide to move to Arizona. Was that the "right" choice?

Certainly. You embrace the cacti – figuratively, please. You enjoy the mountains, the desert, the hot weather, the laid-back life style. Yes, you can be glad you moved. What a good choice!

To make decisions and take action, you need first to realize you can make either choice work out for you. Once you have that confidence, then you won't be shackled by indecision and doubt. No matter what choice you make, you can discover its positives and make them work for you. With that attitude in place, you then do your homework, gathering information and opinions. You set your priorities, and then you trust your impulses. Throughout the entire process, you don't want to take yourself too seriously. Lighten up a little and enjoy the fact that at least you have choices. That's where you sense your power. Without choices you truly have no power. So even if you're having some difficulty deciding which way to go, at least you have options before you, and *you* can choose.

Principle 10

Imagine the worst as a way of fighting fear.

You picture the airplane losing power at 35,000 feet and free falling for what feels like hours. You envision yourself walking through a cave filled with snakes and bats. You see yourself crossing a canyon on a rope bridge. While you imagine these things, you attempt to breath deeply and remain calm. This approach, called "flooding," attempts to help you gain an inner calm despite the awful event around you.

To try "flooding" with your fear, you need to sit quietly and relax your body. Go through a relaxation exercise to quiet yourself. Then begin imagining the event you fear. See it in great detail. Stay with it. Enter it. If it gets too stressful for you, then return to your breathing and make another effort to relax your body. Then do this flooding exercise again the next day and the next day and the next. You're attempting to link your state of relaxation to the awful experience. You're also seeing the situation differently and will likely begin changing your beliefs about the situation to less dramatic thoughts.

This exercise is often used by psychotherapists as a way of helping people reduce their fears. If you have trouble doing this alone, invite someone to help you. That person can give you support and prompt the image you're working with by describing it for you. Remember, the goal here is to change your *view* of the situation. By staying in it, at least in your mind, you give yourself the chance to get a little more familiar and comfortable with the situation, thus reducing your fear.

Take Definite Action Steps

> **Principle 11**
>
> **Act despite your fears.**

You cannot wait for your fear to dissolve *before* you take action. Were that the case, the world would come to a complete standstill. You realize the fear is there, but you must still go ahead and act. Bill had been in a mild car accident, side-swiped by an 18-wheel truck. After that he couldn't get himself to drive on expressways. He'd panic every time a truck came near. After working on his thinking for a while, he decided the only way to deal with this fear was to get out on the road. On his first attempt, Bill sat in the back seat and his wife drove. The second time out he worked his way to the passenger seat in front. After considerable stress, he began to notice his fear lessening. After a number of trips with his wife driving, Bill finally got behind the wheel himself, and through more courageous work, forcing himself to act against his fear, he was able to drive comfortably on expressways.

So, too, with you. You need to face your fear. Recognize it there, eating a little hole in you. Think it through. Challenge it with new thoughts. Then act on it. Get on the airplane. Hike down the Grand Canyon. Change jobs. Have the baby. Buy the computer. Confront your co-worker. Talk with you spouse about sex. Show affection to that special person. Ride the city bus. Take the evening class. Put the addition on the house. Do all these things, if the only thing stopping you is your fear. If you have collected the information and feel comfortable with your decision to take action, then do it – even if your fear tries to block the path.

In smaller fears of the more neurotic type, taking action is essential to breaking the power of the fear. People who fear open spaces such as shopping malls need to force themselves to walk on through. People who fear they left a light on in the house need to force themselves to act against their compulsion to return and check. People afraid of what others think need to force themselves to act despite others' reactions.

When you don't act on your fears, you then feel controlled by them. You feel helpless and powerless. In such a state you develop a new, deeper fear, the fear of vulnerability. If you have no power, you become vulnerable to the forces of the world around you. Without power you live defenseless in a world that can harm you. So don't let your fears stop you from acting. Call up all the courage you can. And take action.

Principle 12

Know when to act and when not to act on your fears.

In the last section it may have sounded like I was encouraging you to always act against your fears. There are times when it's safer not to act. At times your fears are telling you to back away and not get involved. The prudence principle applies: Do not take action when your fear clearly signals danger to you or others. Of course, whenever you're afraid, you sense some danger. The trick is to determine which dangers are real and which are exaggerated, interfering with your well-being.

Some fears clearly interfere with your well-being and should be acted against. You might fear going to the doctor to find out what your cholesterol level is, so you put it off. It's a greater danger to put it off than to go. In this case you need to overcome your fear and go. The same is true of going to the dentist, taking a final exam, talking to your boss about a well-deserved raise and driving your car in the city. If you're afraid of intimacy, it's generally better to overcome your fear by acting in intimate ways with your spouse, lover or children.

On the other hand, some fears can be entertained and allowed to dictate your behavior. If you're afraid of heights, you need not sky dive or stand at the edge of cliffs. That fear may not interfere in your life in any significant way. You may fear dogs. When you see a large German Shepherd loose on the street, you may choose to walk in the opposite direction. Fine. You may fear going to jail. Your fear keeps you from robbing the bank. This is called "prudent fear" because it keeps you safe from harm.

When you feel fear, you generally seek to back away from a situation. That's the knee-jerk reaction. But ask yourself if avoiding the situation keeps you safer than going into the situation. If you answer "Yes, avoidance protects me from a greater danger than engaging the situation," then back away. If you answer "No, avoidance makes matters only worse," then enter the situation even though you feel the fear.

Principle 13

You reduce your anxiety as you develop your interpersonal relationships.

If your deepest anxiety results from the experience of *separation,* then the antidote to that anxiety is the formation of community. Your fear naturally urges you to avoid and back away from situations and people. That fear triples itself when you give in to it and withdraw. Not only are you afraid, but you are alone in your fear. Plus you are afraid of being alone! Now it's really getting complex.

The answer to anxiety is to share your life with others. Even though you feel like withdrawing when you're afraid, try moving toward another. Open up to that person and share your concern and fear. I know that exposing fear makes you feel vulnerable. It makes you think you're weak. You should be able to handle your fears and worries, you think. You shouldn't need support. Nonsense. Keeping to yourself increases your fear. It isolates you and reinforces your deepest fear – the fear of living your life alone.

Here's a good place to take the risk of opening yourself to another. Push yourself on this one. Don't hedge, saying you'll take care of it alone. Maybe you can this time. But try sharing with another and feel his support, and sense that you're not in this alone. Let others have the chance to care about you in an active way. Friends want to be there for each other when the need is there. Right now, you need a friend. So go to that person and open up your fears.

Principle 14

Go toward people to give support and help to them. Doing so reduces your own fears.

If you give to another, you focus on that person. You draw your attention away from you and direct it to the other. By doing so, you de-power your own fears. In a dramatic instance you might jump into the swimming hole to save a child without considering the danger to you. If you were afraid of water and focused on the danger to you, you wouldn't jump in to get the child. But by focusing on the well-being of the child, you "forget" your own fear as you give yourself to the child's safety.

The key principle, applied throughout this **Life Skills Series**, fits here: *You give power to what you focus on.* Concentrate on your fear of water, and you stay on the shore and possibly watch the child drown. Focus on the safety of the child, and you jump into the water and save the child's life.

When you give to others, you cannot do so simply to get something in return. Such giving actually increases your fear, because you're gambling. You're betting that if you give something to this person, you will get back equal to or more than you gave. Waiters and waitresses, barbers, taxi drivers and caddies all give in order to get. They work hard to please you, then expect your tip to be generous. They experience that moment of anxiety when they walk off and in private check the amount you gave. Quickly their fear turns to joy or disappointment and anger.

Although you cannot love altruistically all the time, you can move in that direction through conscious effort. By loving and giving to people for *their* good rather than your own, you, in fact, receive much. One of the key gifts you gain in return is the reduction of fear and the increase of peace and confidence in yourself.

You have much to give others. You can give them your quiet listening, your advice (when they really ask for it) and your time. You can give them your delight over *their* successes (that's a hard one for frightened and insecure people). You can give them praise, respect, affection, hope and, perhaps most importantly, you can give them *courage.* Standing with someone, supporting and en*couraging,* allows that person to overcome the fear in his or her life. Strangely, by helping to free that person from his or her fear, you de-power your own fears. You give courage to the other, and you receive courage in your act of giving. You always receive in giving to others as long as you don't give only to get something back. Give to give, and let yourself be surprised by what happens to you in return.

Learn to Relax

Easy to say if you're not in a state of panic. Oh, sure, just relax. Everything will be fine. This piece of advice makes sense, certainly. If you just relaxed and took it easy when you were in the frightening situation, all would probably work out well. But to tell someone to relax when panic has already struck seems like saying "Don't be sad" when someone dies. So, what to do?

> **Principle 15**
>
> **Practice relaxation exercises to reduce fear.**

First, I want to admit that trying to relax when your anxiety and fear are already in full bloom is futile – unless you have been *practicing* relaxation for a significant period of time before the fear hit.

If you practice relaxing when you're not particularly stressed or fearful, you have a good chance of experiencing relaxation. If you keep on practicing, you gradually anchor to your techniques a state of peace and calm. Then when you come up against the big fears and anxieties of life, you are able to turn to your well-practiced techniques and employ them on the spot. The effect of such practice is that the state of peace and quiet attached to your relaxation processes comes to you at those times of fear. You are able to relax while you're frightened, but only if you practice beforehand.

And I don't mean just for a week. It usually takes months of regular practice to create the ability to bring relaxation to bear on your fears. I explain more about relaxing, how to do it, and what to expect in the **Life Skills Series** book *Managing Stress*.

> **Principle 16**
>
> **Reduce fear by combining relaxation with action.**

What I am about to describe is called "systematic desensitization." It's a process used by many psychotherapists to help people manage their phobias – fears they have over specific objects.

To break down your fears in this systematic way, you begin by engaging regularly in relaxation exercises. Do these exercises at least four or five times a week. Every day is preferable. After doing this for six weeks, you begin taking action.

You identify your fear. Let's say you're afraid of swimming. You want to overcome your fear of water because you live in a hot weather climate and you would also love to go on a cruise. So you need to overcome your fear of being in water over your head.

You make a list of 20 steps, from least frightening to most frightening, namely, being alone in water over your head. The least frightening step is seeing a lake from your car. Next least frightening is standing outside your car, 100 yards from the shore. Next is standing at the shore. Next is putting your foot in the water. And so on. Each step creates more anxiety.

Once you have your list, you begin by going through your relaxation exercises. When you feel relaxed and comfortable, you take step one and *imagine* yourself sitting in the car looking at the lake. If you feel any anxiety, drop that picture and return to your relaxation exercise. If you can continue seeing the picture of the lake from your car and stay relaxed, then you have mastered step one. You go on to step two – seeing the lake from 100 yards away. As you enter each step, attempt to imagine it while staying relaxed. If you can't do it, return to the step before, where you could feel relaxed.

After you get through all the steps in your mind, you begin to go through the steps live and in color. You drive your car out to the lake and look at it while doing your relaxation exercises. You keep taking it step by step until you're out there swimming in water over your head. You can do it. This approach has been very effective with people who have specific fears. It takes time and work. But if it's worth it to you to overcome a particular fear, then I would suggest this systematic approach.

Well, now you know the tools for fighting your fear and overcoming anxiety. You want to:
1. Become aware of your fear and what causes it.
2. Learn to think in non-fearful ways.
3. Take definite action steps.
4. Learn to relax.

These four steps are your recipe to reducing the anxiety, fear and worry in your life. I know you're motivated to conquer your fears. I wish for you courage and all the support you can get from your friends and loved ones. Strengthening the skill of overcoming fear will give you a sense of freedom and peace of mind you have not known before. Without fear your ability to love life and others will know no bounds. Without fear you set yourself on the path to living life to its fullest.

Chapter Four

Developing this Skill with Others

Working on your fears with another person or with a group helps you overcome those fears. Finding support and help from others in developing this skill means you have already risked and overcome the fear of sharing your fears. In the group or with your friend you know security and concern, two feelings that displace fear. But you can do much more with one another than just give support and concern. You can work with each other in specific ways to overcome fear. Here are some directions to get you started with each other or a group:

Step 1

Begin by discussing the big anxieties, namely death and separation. Talk about your experiences, beliefs and feelings around the deaths of your loved ones and around your own death. Then discuss what you believe happens after death. Is there another life or not? If so, what do you think it will be like?

Step 2

Have a discussion about the "voided heart" experience. Do you have a voided heart? If yes, how have you attempted to fill that up? Can you accept the fact that it will never be completely filled? What are the implications of your voided heart today for you?

Step 3

Now have a discussion about *meaning* and *purpose* in life. Where do you find meaning? in work? in relationships? in God? How balanced are these three pillars? What would happen if your most important pillar crumbled?

Step 4

Having discussed the big anxieties, turn your attention to your specific fears. Identify them and write them down. Share them with each other and notice which ones you have in common.

Step 5

Take a particular fear you share and discuss your beliefs that create the fear. Next take a fear that you don't have in common and again identify the beliefs you have that keep that fear alive.

Step 6

Now take those same fears and together challenge your beliefs with new, more realistic, less dramatic beliefs. Write these new beliefs out so they are specific and clear. Use them throughout the week to challenge your fear.

Step 7

After mentally challenging your fearful beliefs, decide on

actions that make you enter what you fear. Support one another in this step, because it takes courage to act against your fears.

Step 8

Do relaxation exercises together. Each person in the group could bring one or two exercises and teach the others. Eventually get comfortable with one or the other exercise and stick with it. Practice relaxation with the group. You can start each session with a brief relaxation exercise.

Step 9

Take a specific fear that one or a number of group members has and do "systematic desensitization" as I described above. This is a particularly effective process when done with another or with a group.

Conclusion

Working with another or with a group on your fears could go on for a long time, because overcoming fear lends itself so well to a group process. You can go into as many fears as you want, discussing their various angles, searching out the thought patterns that cause the fears and creating new thought patterns that reduce your fears. The support you get from one another is invaluable. I strongly encourage you to join forces with a friend or a group in developing the skill of overcoming fear. As this skill grows in you, you will discover that your own heart is filled with the energy to risk. We call it courage. With courage comes action. With action comes a sense of power, the power to live your life to its fullest.

Appendix

Review of Principles for Overcoming Fear

1. Information increases your ability to predict outcomes. Predictability reduces fear.
2. Create an attitude of courage by viewing yourself as competent.
3. Focusing on who you are rather than what you do helps reduce anxiety.
4. Make an act of faith in your own nurturing power to handle your "voided heart."
5. Search for answers to the ultimate questions of life.
6. Recognize and challenge dramatic and catastrophic thinking.
7. Make sure you observe data in a calm and accurate way.
8. Insist on and practice thinking in positive, objective and calming ways.
9. Gain a sense of personal power in your life.
10. Imagine the worst as a way of fighting fear.
11. Act despite your fears.

12. Know when to act and when not to act on your fears.
13. You reduce your anxiety as you develop your interpersonal relationships.
14. Go toward people to give support and help to them. Doing so reduces your own fears.
15. Practice relaxation exercises to reduce fear.
16. Reduce fear by combining relaxation with action.